BOOK ANALYSIS

By Maria Aalto

Song of Solomon

BY TONI MORRISON

TONI MORRISON

AMERICAN WRITER

- **Born in Lorain, Ohio in 1931.**
- **Notable works:**
  - *The Bluest Eye* (1970), novel
  - *Beloved* (1987), novel
  - *A Mercy* (2008), novel

Toni Morrison is an award-winning writer and a Nobel Laureate. She is widely considered to be one of the most important American writers of our time.

Morrison is a writer of novels, short stories, plays and non-fiction. She is also an editor and a professor emeritus at Princeton University. She has received various prizes for her work, including the National Book Critics Circle Award for *Song of Solomon*, the Pulitzer Prize for Fiction for *Beloved*, and most notably, the Nobel Prize for Literature in 1993.

She is an African-American writer, and her work explores the experiences of black people in

America. Her success and her status as an intellectual and as a Nobel Laureate mark her out as one of the most influential black American writers of the past decades. Slavery, racial oppression and the experience of being black in America are important elements in her fiction. Other significant themes include family, motherhood and love. Morrison's style is unique: her use of language is poetic, and her use of African-American Vernacular English (AAVE) brings her characters to life.

SONG OF SOLOMON

A NOVEL ABOUT THE AFRICAN-AMERICAN EXPERIENCE IN THE 20TH CENTURY IN THE FORM OF A COMING-OF-AGE STORY

- **Genre:** novel
- **Reference edition:** Morrison, T. (2016) *Song of Solomon*. London: Vintage.
- **1st edition:** 1977
- **Themes:** the African-American experience in the 20th century, racism, violence, family, love, identity, flight as escape

Song of Solomon, which is set between 1931 and 1963, tells the story of, Milkman, a young African-American man who is searching for his identity. Milkman is the son of a wealthy property owner and the grandson of the first coloured doctor in his city. While he does not enjoy the same rights and opportunities as white Americans, he is nevertheless privileged because of his wealthy background. The novel is his coming-of-age story, in which he searches for his place in the African-American community, learns about his family's history and finally learns to care about other people.

The novel explores the experience of being black in America in the 20th century, before the Civil Rights Movement had succeed in obtaining equal rights for black and white Americans. The legacy of slavery, segregation and racism – which still impacts American society today – is explored through the experiences of Milkman's family and other members of his community. The importance of knowing one's past and connecting with the people in one's life are at the heart of this novel.

SUMMARY

ATTEMPTS TO FLY

The novel, which is set in Michigan, opens with Robert Smith, an African-American insurance agent (and, as it is later revealed, a member of a black vigilante/terrorist group) attempting to fly, and plunging to his death. The next day, Macon Dead, also known as Milkman, becomes the first black baby to be born in the Mercy hospital. Milkman's mother, Ruth, is the daughter of the first African-American doctor in the city (who is dead in the present of the novel), but it is the confusion caused by Mr. Smith's leap rather than her status that allows her to give birth in the hospital.

Milkman has two much older sisters: Magdalene called Lena and First Corinthians. Lena and Corinthians' names were chosen randomly from the Bible, just like their paternal grandfather had done with their aunt Pilate. Their father is called Macon Dead like his father (and his son). Macon Dead I received his name because of a mistake made by a drunken Freedman's Bureau official. Macon Dead II is a wealthy property owner, but he is unhappy because of his traumatic childhood, which involved his father being shot dead by white people who were after his property near Danville, Pennsylvania, where he lived as a child, and because of his unhappy marriage. He suspects his wife had an incestuous relationship with her father, and as a result he is abusive towards her. He is also estranged from his sister, Pilate, because he does not approve of her eccentric lifestyle as a bootlegger (and, as it is later revealed, because they quarrelled over a white man whom Macon Dead killed when he and Pilate were hiding in a cave after their father was murdered, and over the gold the dead white man had, which Macon wanted to take and Pilate would not let him, and which he believes she later took).

When Milkman is four, mirroring Mr. Smith's failed attempt to fly (or his suicide), he is disappointed to learn that only birds and aeroplanes fly. His family's life is dull and lacking love. Macon Dead and Ruth's relationship is unhappy, and it impacts the whole family. Ruth seeks comfort in secretly breastfeeding her child well past infancy into childhood, until one day they are discovered by Freddie, the janitor. This is what gives Milkman his nickname.

PILATE AND HER FAMILY

When Milkman is in his early teens, he explores life in his city with his friend Guitar. Guitar is older than Milkman, and from a working-class family. He acts as mentor for Milkman as they go to places like bars and the barbershop. One day Milkman and Guitar visit Milkman's aunt Pilate, with whom he has had no contact since his infancy because his father has forbidden it. Milkman gets to know Pilate, her daughter Reba and Reba's daughter Hagar. He later begins a relationship with Hagar. When Milkman and Guitar first come to visit Pilate, they want to know if it is true that she does not have a navel. Indeed, she does not, which has caused her to be rejected by many people, but which also sets her apart as an exceptional individual who has learned to live her life as she wants to instead of worrying about what people think.

One evening when Milkman is 14, he defends his

mother by hitting Macon Dead back when he hits her. Macon Dead then tells his son why he hits her, explaining that when her father died, he found her lying naked next to his body. Years later, when Milkman confronts her, she denies this. She explains that she was not naked, and that she felt that her father was the only one who truly loved her.

KILLING IN THE NAME OF LOVE AND VENGEANCE

When Milkman is an adult in his early 30s, he still lives with his parents, as do his sisters. He also works for his father. His life is comfortable but lacks direction and meaning. His is still in a (not very committed) relationship with Hagar. Now, after about 12 years, he decides to break it off. Hagar is left heartbroken, desperate and angry. She seems to lose her mind after being abandoned and tries to kill Milkman once every month.

Milkman's friendship with Guitar remains important to him, but their relationship begins to change. While Milkman lives a privileged, relatively carefree life and does not think much about other people, Guitar becomes more serious, and angry at white people. He finally confesses to Milkman that he is a member of vigilante (or terrorist) group which seeks to avenge the deaths of black people killed by white people by killing (innocent) white people in a similar fashion as the black victims were killed. Milkman tells Guitar that killing innocents is wrong, but Guitar does not think that white people, generally speaking, are innocent. Although Milkman and Guitar disagree, they remain friends.

When Macon Dead hears one day that his sister has her 'inheritance' in a bag at her house, he becomes convinced that it is the gold she would not let him take from the white man he killed. He tells this to Milkman and they plan to steal it from her. Milkman invites Guitar to help him and promises him a share of it. They steal the bag, but instead of gold they find human bones in it. Milkman and Guitar are arrested, but Macon Dead and Pilate intervene to have them released. Pilate tells the police that the bones are those of her dead husband, whom she could not afford to bury. In fact, she had gone back to the cave to get the bones of the man her brother killed because her dead father, who repeatedly appears to Pilate, had told her that they could not leave the body behind. Pilate believes that one is responsible for the life one takes.

CONNECTING WITH THE PAST

Macon Dead believes that the gold is still in the cave. Milkman, who wants to be independent from his father, decides to go alone to look for the cave in Pennsylvania. When he arrives in Danville, he meets people who knew his father, Pilate and/or their grandfather. He finds out that his grandfather was respected and admired by his community. He is told that his grandfather was murdered by white people who wanted his farm. Milkman meets Circe, the incredibly old midwife who delivered his father and Pilate, and who helped them after their father was killed. She tells him that his grandfather was originally called Jake and that his grandmother, who died just before Pilate was born, was an Indian called Sing. He also learns that his grandfather's body had resurfaced after it was buried, and that it had been thrown into the cave Macon Dead and

Pilate took shelter in. Milkman goes to search the cave but does not find the gold or his grandfather's bones. It seems that the bones of the white man were no longer in the cave by the time Pilate went to search for them, and what she has are actually her father's remains.

Milkman is intrigued by his family's past, and he decides to go to Virginia, where his grandparents came from. He arrives in Shalimar, where after some initial trouble with the residents he is accepted. He finds a relative of his grandmother and finds out that his great-grandfather was Solomon, who was said to have escaped slavery by flying away, but leaving his wife and children behind. It is said that he tried to take his son Jake with him, but Jake had fallen down, and was found by Heddy, Sing's mother, who then raised him. Later, Sing and Jake ran away together.

Milkman also discovers that Guitar has been following him, with the intention of killing him because he believes that Milkman has found the gold, but does not intend to share it. Milkman tries to tell Guitar that there was no gold in the cave, but Guitar does not believe him.

TAKING A LEAP

After discovering his family's past and learning about himself on his journey, Milkman is eager to return home to tell his father and Pilate what he has discovered. He has become more compassionate and understands his family better now. However, when Milkman arrives home, he discovers that Hagar has died of a broken heart, and Pilate is angry at him. He accepts responsibility for Hagar's death. He tells his father and Pilate about everything he has discovered.

Finally, Pilate and Milkman return to Shalimar to burry Milkman's grandfather. Just after they have finished, Pilate dies from a bullet Guitar had intended for Milkman. After laying his aunt to rest, inspired by his family's history, Milkman leaps towards Guitar, who has lowered his gun. The novel has an open ending, as it is not clear what happens to Milkman and Guitar.

CHARACTER STUDY

MILKMAN DEAD

Milkman is a privileged young African-American man. He was given his nickname because his mother nursed him longer than many people find 'normal'. He is spoiled, and initially does not care much about others' needs. He has been pampered by the women in his life and has never had to do much for himself or for other people. He is initially unable to form meaningful relationships with others because of this. He is dependent on his wealthy father, but eager to become independent. Milkman grows as a person when he goes to the South and finds, instead of the gold he was looking for, his family's past. As a small boy he dreamed of flying and was disappointed to learn that "only birds and airplanes could fly" (p. 11). Consequently, when he learns that his great-grandfather, Solomon, was said to have escaped slavery by flying away, he is at first very excited and proud of him. Later, however, he realises that when Solomon flew away, as inspiring as it may be in terms of escaping the cruelty of slavery, he left his wife and his children behind (pp. 413-414). This realisation is pivotal, as it means that Milkman has become aware of responsibility towards others. He accepts the responsibility for Hagar's death and becomes more compassionate. This realisation, along with his newfound understanding of the importance of his family's past, changes him profoundly. In addition to discovering his identity, he now values his family and feels part of it.

MACON DEAD

Macon Dead is Milkman's father. He is defined by his childhood traumas and by his unhappy marriage. He only seems happy when he talks about his childhood, before his father was murdered. His father was an illiterate but successful farmer, who was proud of his farm. The loss of his father and of the family's farm were deeply traumatic for Macon Dead, who now lives gathering material wealth. His marriage to Milkman's mother is deeply unhappy because he believes that she had an inappropriate relationship with her father. He constantly tries to become richer and more successful, but it does not really make him happy. In the end, when Milkman returns from his trip, he stays essentially the same, but he is pleased to hear everything that his son has discovered.

RUTH FOSTER DEAD

Ruth is Milkman's mother. She an unhappy woman, stuck in an unhappy marriage. She is lonely, and feels as if the only person who really cared for her was her now-dead father. She craves love, but does not find it in her marriage. She seeks comfort in breastfeeding her son longer than usual and visiting her father's grave at night. She does both of these things in secret, which shows that she knows she would be judged by most people for what she does. Her son too initially judges her, but finally learns to feel compassion for the suffering of both of his parents.

PILATE

Pilate is Milkman's aunt and Macon Dead's sister. She is an exceptional, eccentric woman. She has suffered a number of losses and rejections, such as losing both of her parents as a child, and being rejected from a number of communities because she is seen as unnatural because she does not have a navel. In spite of this, she is strong, independent, kind and caring. In fact, her struggles have thought her both the importance of living her life as she wishes to, and the value of love and compassion. She is the strongest and most empathic character in the novel. For example, she protects her daughter from a violent man, but without really hurting him. She also comes to help Milkman and Guitar when they are arrested, even though she knows that they had tried to steal from her. She is an important person in Milkman's life, as she is the family member from whom he learns the most, and the person he goes to see first when he comes back from his travels. She has always loved and protected her nephew, who, although he has always liked her, only understands her true value when he is transformed by his discoveries and realisations. When Pilate is dying, he understands what makes her so special to him: "Now he realises why he loved her so. Without ever leaving the ground, she could fly" (p. 419).

REBA

Reba is Pilate's daughter and Hagar's mother. Reba is lucky and wins prizes at games without trying to, but usually gives away what she wins, generally to men. She has had several relationships, none of which have developed into anything serious despite her yearning for love.

HAGAR

Hagar is Reba's daughter. Although she is not wealthy, she is spoiled (even if not in the same way as Milkman), as her mother and her grandmother try to provide her with everything she asks for. She has a long relationship with Milkman, who never really commits to her. When Milkman decides he no longer wants a relationship with her, she becomes angry and desperate. She then tries to kill him once every month, without ever succeeding in harming him. After the last failed attempt, she becomes ill because of her sorrow and finally dies. She represents a woman whose love is excessive and who cannot function without the man she loves. Her behaviour mirrors that of her great-grandmother, Ryna, who lost her mind after her husband, Solomon, flew away. Even though Hagar's love is excessive, Milkman learns – too late for Hagar – to have compassion for her when he realises that flying away means leaving someone behind.

GUITAR

Guitar is Milkman's best friend, and finally also his enemy, both at the same time. Guitar is from a working-class family and has had a traumatic childhood. His father was killed in a sawmill accident at work, and Guitar is angry at his father's white boss, who did not handle the incident with enough respect for the family. He is also generally angry at white people for all the racial oppression in America. He joins a vigilante/terrorist organisation which kills white people to avenge the deaths of murdered black people. What shocks Milkman the most when he finds out about this is that they do not kill the people who committed the crimes, but other white people, similar to the black victims. In fact, they attempt to copy the original crime as faithfully as possible. Milkman says that killing innocents is wrong, but Guitar thinks that no white person is truly innocent. While Milkman and Guitar stay friends after this conversation, it changes their relationship. Their friendship is finally shaken even more when Guitar becomes convinced that Milkman has found the gold and is not sharing it with him, and decides to kill him.

Curiously enough, this does not entirely end their friendship. Guitar warns Milkman of his intentions because he still sees him as a friend. Moreover, their relationship is complex and resists simple classifications, as can be observed from the following quote: "Would you save my life or would you take it? Guitar was exceptional. To both questions he could answer yes" (p. 412).

ANALYSIS

AFRICAN-AMERICAN EXPERIENCES

Song of Solomon explores the lives of African-American people and the experience of being black in America. While most of the events in the novel take place in the 20th century, the investigation of these experiences stretches further back in history as the past of Milkman's family is treated as crucial to understanding who they are. Slavery, segregation and racism in America are deep traumas that impact many aspects of the lives of African-Americans. Morrison discusses these traumas, but also shows the beauty and strength of African-American culture. Morrison uses legends, myths, biblical references and allusions to African-American music and to the Civil Rights Movement to create a complex novel that celebrates African-American culture while also investigating its hardships.

RACIAL INEQUALITY AND AFRICAN-AMERICAN EMPOWERMENT

As the events in the novel take place in the year 1963 and before, black Americans in *Song of Solomon* live in a country where they are considered as second-class citizens. Milkman's family's history includes slavery, violence and racial oppression. One of the most blatant examples of racial violence in the novel is the murder of Milkman's grandfather. Other, subtler, but nevertheless harmful, wrongdoings include not allowing black women to give birth in the Mercy hospital, and the carelessness of the Freedman's Bureau official whose mistake gave the first Macon Dead his name, and as a consequence lost his original name from the records. Names and knowing the names of family members carry a symbolic significance in this novel, as these names are connected with identity, and the names of ancestors are connected with the family's past. Disregarding the importance of Macon Dead's – Jake's – name is thus harmful for the whole family. Milkman's search for his family's past and his discovery of the names of his grandparents and great-grandparents is thus empowering.

The racism in the novel is set alongside black empowerment. This is done by evoking African (American) folklore, African-American culture and the Civil Rights Movement. The legend of the Flying African, which "forms a part of the racial memory of people of African descent" (Hope Scott 2007: 27) is explored in an innovative fashion in the novel. The legend tells of slaves escaping slavery by flying home to Africa. Flight as escape is also significant in Morrison's novel. However, in the novel, Solomon escapes slavery alone, leaving his wife and his family behind, which problematises the possible consequences of escaping. Pilate provides a solution, because, in Milkman's words, "Without ever leaving the ground, she could fly" (p. 419) (see also Dubek 2015: 105). Flying without leaving the ground not only solves the problem of those left behind, but also fits the context in which most of the African descents are American, and thus already home, even if they might feel the need to escape the racial oppression.

Dubek (2015) argues that Morrison alludes to the Civil Rights Movement and Martin Luther King and Malcom X in the novel. She points to the consonants in Milkman, "MLKman" (Dubek 2015: 96) to show the allusion, and demonstrates that while Milkman, who initially was rather uninterested in other people, is not an uncomplicated image of Martin Luther King, some aspects of him, such as associating him with dreaming, do fit the description. Dubek also draws parallels between Guitar, who is far more radical in his approach to racial injustice than his friend, and Malcom X (*ibid.*: 100). These, and numerous other allusions (see Dubek 2015 for more information) to the black resistance of white oppression, are important because they show the strength African-Americans. Together with the numerous references to African-American culture and legends in the novel, they act as tools for empowerment.

BIBLICAL REFERENCES

In addition to the cultural references mentioned, there are several meaningful biblical allusions in the novel, but as Wierzbinski points out, they do not amount to a neat pattern that would explain the whole novel (Wierzbinski 2005: 126-127). Some of the biblical allusions, such as the biblical names given to the children in the Dead family, permit only partial parallels to be drawn between the novel and the Bible, and some seem downright ironic, such as the name given to Pilate. Wierzbinski maintains that Pontius Pilate and Pilate of the *Song of Solomon* "could not be more unlike" (*ibid.*: 127), and continues to observe that out of all of the charters in the novel, Pilate is the most like Christ, as she is loving, protective and ready to humble her self for the sake of others, even when they have done her wrong (like Milkman and Guitar have). The subtle irony of this character's name adds a further layer of meaning to the multifaceted novel.

Another obvious biblical reference in the novel is the title, which refers to the Song of Solomon in the Old Testament. The biblical text is about marital love, and as Wierzbinski demonstrates, love between men and woman is also central to Morrison's novel, with the difference that there are no happy marital unions present in the novel (*ibid.*: 135-136). Morrison thus investigates the love relationships, and their difficulties, such as men failing to commit to their partners. Milkman's transformation offers some hope, because he finally understands his responsibility towards the women in his life, even if this comes too late for Hagar. He also expresses a wish to find a companion like his aunt at the moment of her death: "There must be another one like you" he whispered to her. "There's got to be at least one more woman like you"" (p. 419).

FAMILY

Family and the importance of family ties are essential parts of the novel. Knowing the names of one's ancestors, knowing one's family's history and feeling connected to one's family are brought forward as vital. In the beginning, Milkman is selfish and uninterested in his family. However, by connecting with his family's past, he discovers his identity, which underlines the importance of his knowing 'his people'.

COMING-OF-AGE STORY

The exploration of the themes discussed takes the form of a coming-of-age story. Milkman, who is initially spoiled and disconnected from his family and his community, searches for his identity and eventually comes to better understand himself, his family, and his fellow African-Americans. The novel describes his journey from a little boy to a young man, and finally to an empowered individual. Milkman's journey to the American South is the reversal of the common narrative of African-Americans moving to the North. Milkman makes the journey back to the South and back to his family's past. He sets out to find gold, but finally comes back home with something valuable on an emotional level: his identity, and understanding and empathy towards his family and his community.

STYLE

Song of Solomon's style is remarkable. Morrison's writing is rhythmical and flowing, and full of allusions to African-American myths, culture and history. The most important stylistic devices Morrison uses are poetic language, African-American Vernacular English (AAVE) and third person narrative that changes focus from one character to another.

The novel is written as a third person narrative which focuses mainly on Milkman. This permits the reader to observe how he experiences his coming-of-age journey. However, the point of focus is not fixed on Milkman, which means that the reader gets a broader perspective of the events in the novel, as the focus moves from one character to another.

One of the most remarkable stylistic features of the novel is its poetic style, which amplifies the impact of its content. The poetic devices that Morrison uses are repetition, poetic images and rhythm and rhyme. Observe, for example, the musicality of the following passage describing Milkman's contact with the people who knew his grandfather in Danville: "Grab this land! Take it, hold it, my brothers, make it, my brothers, shake it, squeeze it, turn it, twist it, beat it, kick it, kiss it, whip it, stomp it, dig it, plow it, seed it, reap it, rent it, buy it, sell it, own it, build it, multiply it, and pass it on – can you hear me? Pass it on!" (p. 239). Dubek connects this type of passage with African-American music, and more specifically with the gospel performances of Solomon Burke (Dubek 2015: 99). This is therefore another way in which African-American culture is celebrated in this novel.

Another important stylistic feature of Morrison's writing which is also connected with African-

American culture is the use of AAVE. Observe, for example, the grammatical structure of the following quote from a dialogue between Pilate and Guitar (Pilate is speaking), particularly the verb forms (and the absence of the verb to be): "I ain't the one with the wants. You the one want something" (p. 45). Hope Scott explains that Morrison affirms the role of African-American language in her literary art, as a manifestation of Black Art (Hope Scott 2007: 26-27). Her literary art brings her characters to life, and her language use affirms their identities. The stylistic elements of the novel support the exploration of African-American experiences, both the necessary investigation of the traumas of racial oppression, and the celebration of African-American culture.

FURTHER REFLECTION

SOME QUESTIONS TO THINK ABOUT...

- Discuss the different examples of racial injustice in the novel.
- How would you interpret the novel's open ending?
- How would you interpret the novel's title?
- Discuss the friendship between Milkman and Guitar, and how their relationship evolves in the novel.
- In your opinion, why does Pilate come to help Milkman and Guitar after they have stolen from her? What does this act tell us about her?
- Names are given special attention in this novel. Why do you think that is? What is the connection between names and identity implied in the novel?
- Knowing his family's past helps Milkman understand his family's present. Describe the ways in which Morrison connects the past

and the present in the novel, and discuss their meanings.

- Discuss the repeated notion of flying in the novel. What is its symbolic meaning?

We want to hear from you!
Leave a comment on your online library
and share your favourite books on social media!

FURTHER READING

REFERENCE EDITION

- Morrison, T. (2016) *Song of Solomon*. London: Vintage.

REFERENCE STUDIES

- Dubek, L. (2015) "Pass It On!": Legacy and the Freedom Struggle in Toni Morrison's *Song of Solomon. The Southern Quarterly* 52(2). pp. 90-109.

- Hope Scott, J. (2007) *Song of Solomon* and T*ar Baby:* The subversive role of language and the carnivalesque. In Tally, J. ed. *The Cambridge Companion to Toni Morrison.* Cambridge: Cambridge University Press. pp. 26-42.

- Jimoh, A. (2002) Toni Morrison: Biography (2002). *The Literary Encyclopedia.* 88.

- Wierzbinski, J. (2005) Biblical References in Toni Morrison's *Song of Solomon. Onoma.* 40. pp. 125-143.

ADDITIONAL SOURCES

- Tally, J. ed. (2007) *The Cambridge Companion to Toni Morrison*. Cambridge: Cambridge University Press.

MORE FROM BRIGHTSUMMARIES.COM

- Reading guide – *Beloved* by Toni Morrison.

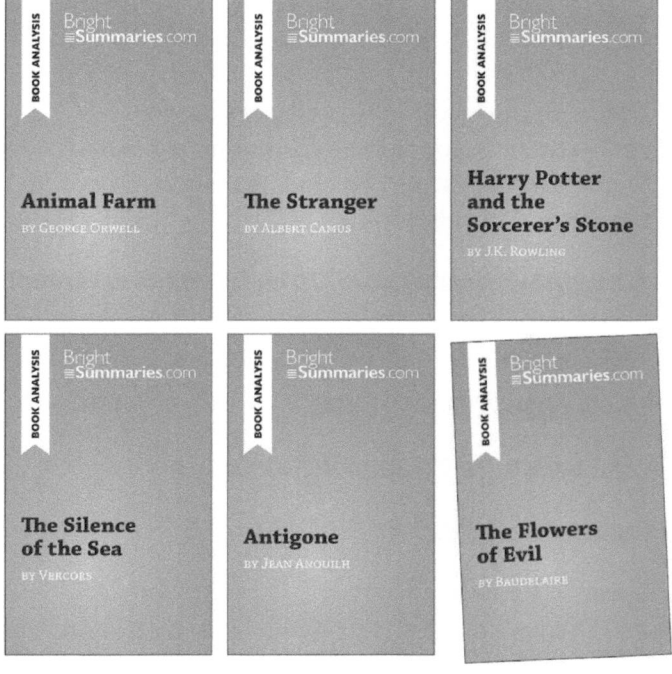

www.brightsummaries.com

Ebook EAN: 9782808015493

Paperback EAN: 9782808015509

Legal Deposit: D/2018/12603/533

Cover: © Primento

Digital conception by Primento, the digital partner of publishers.